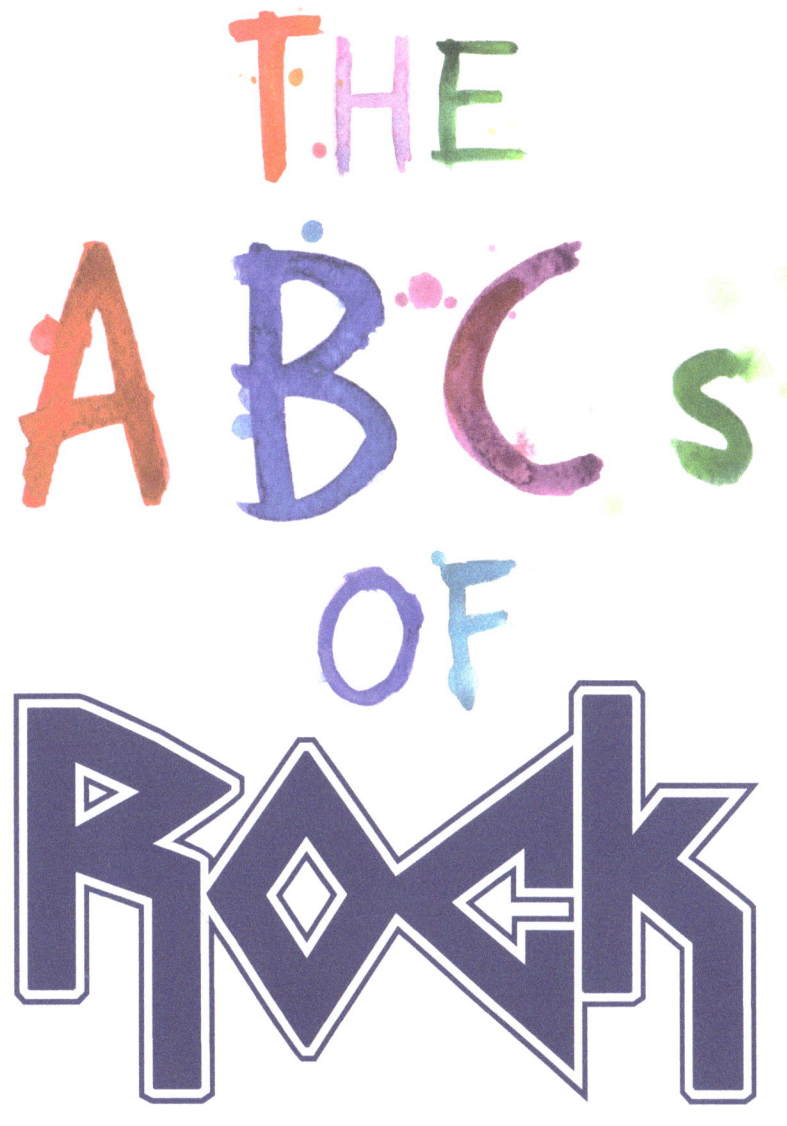

Belongs to _____

Copyright ©2021 By Randy Diderrich

All rights reserved. No part of this book may be reproduced or transmitted in any form or by any means, electronic or mechanical, including photocopying, recording, or by any information storage and retrieval system, without permission in writing from the copyright owner. This is a work of fiction. Names, characters, places and incidents either are the product of the author's imagination or are used fictitiously, and any resemblance to any actual persons, living or dead, events or locales is entirely coincidental.

The ABCs of Rock

Written by Randy Diderrich
Illustrated by Elizabeth Bagby
Layout by Kyle Kummer
Elizabeth Bagby cover photo by Johnny Knight

ISBN: 978-1945907-97-5

Published by Nico 11 Publishing & Design
www.nico11publishing.com
Michael Nicloy, Publisher

Quantity orders may be purchased directly from the publisher.
Send requests to: mike@nico11publishing.com

Printed in the United States of America

THE ABCs OF ROCK

The ABCs of ROCK is dedicated to my son, Nicholas, and my wife, Georgann, both of whom inspire me every day!

Thanks to Liz for her AMAZING paintings and Mike for supporting the project.

...is for Amplifier, making it loud!

J ...is for Jamming.

Where the song starts.

K ...is for keyboard.

Synth sounds are neat.

THE SOFT SUBWAY

Mass Appeel

...is for New Record.

These tracks are brand new!

O ...is for Organ,

keyboard times four.

P ...is for Picks.

You'll always need more.

...is for Quarter Note.
Four on the floor.

...is for Xylophone, mallets and bells.

to finally get some sleep.